GET OVER IT!

GETTING PAST YOUR PAST,
MOVING ON TO YOUR FUTURE

DARRELL CARTER

WESTBOW
PRESS
A DIVISION OF THOMAS NELSON

WestBow Press books may be ordered through booksellers or by contacting:

WestBow Press
A Division of Thomas Nelson
1663 Liberty Drive
Bloomington, IN 47403
www.westbowpress.com
1-(866) 928-1240

ISBN: 978-1-4497-4408-3 (sc)
ISBN: 978-1-4497-5907-0 (e)

Library of Congress Control Number: 2012905100

Printed in the United States of America

WestBow Press rev. date: 07/30/2012

To all who are dealing with past or present issues or struggling with future aspirations: press forward, my friends. Be all that God has created, called, and ordained you to be. My prayers are with you, and may God's grace be with you in all that you do. Be strong in the power of our Lord Christ Jesus, and succeed.

What lies behind us and what lies before us are tiny matters compared to what lies within us.

~ Ralph Waldo Emerson

Acknowledgments

First and foremost, I thank God, from whom all blessings flow. I must say that it is only by the grace of God that this book has been completed. I am who I am today through my Lord and Savior Jesus Christ, who died for me and strengthens me daily.

I also would like to thank my mother, Essie Carter, who has been my confidante and strongest supporter in all that I do. I thank my pastor, Leslie Howell, for his leadership and encouragement to go forward; he is there when I need a listening ear, a sounding board, a friend, and a mentor. He constantly reminds me, "Don't be intimidated by other people's issues (abilities, success, or failures). Just do your best." When you think about it, you cannot do anything more than your best, and the result of *doing* your best is that everything will turn out *for* your best.

INTRODUCTION

Every day you need to get out of bed and move into to your future. If what happened yesterday still controls you today, it is time to move past that bondage. Yesterday's chains limit you and keep you from reaching your full potential in your walk with the Lord. This book will help you learn how to get rid of that bondage and move on.

Do not enable or allow *anything* to dictate to you what is going to happen next. Even if something happened only yesterday, leave it there. It is yesterday's news. Get over it!

Do not let anything interfere with what you are anticipating will happen to you on *this* day. Holding on to yesterday will cause you to lose precious time. It will also consume you and delay the manifestation of God's plan for your life.

REPLACE BONDAGE WITH FREEDOM

This book will help you to realize the importance of replacing whatever is holding you back with positive thinking, affirmations, and activities that line up with God's Word and will lead to your personal freedom.

You can find forgiveness in your heart toward others and also toward yourself. You can learn the importance of patting yourself on the back for your achievements and the good things that you do. Then you can set your sights on a positive future and move into it so that you can thrive, prosper, and achieve what you hope for. Your future awaits!

Every day is a new day and a new opportunity. I pray this book helps you to experience all that you can be and to realize God's manifest destiny for your life.

Scriptural Prayers for Breakthrough

The short prayers at the end of this book are based upon Scripture. Take them to heart and own them because they belong to you. Isaiah 55:11 states:

> *So shall my word be that goeth forth out of my mouth: it shall not return unto me void, but it shall accomplish that which I please, and it shall prosper in the thing whereto I sent it.*

Second Corinthians 1:20 informs us that all the promises (Scriptures) of God are "yes and amen" in Christ to the glory of God through us. Count on God to stand by His Word for you. Yes, His Word *is* personal! God *made* it personal—just for you!

> *For God so loved the world, that he gave his only begotten Son, that whosoever believeth in him should not perish, but have everlasting life.*
>
> (John 3:16)

Pray:

Father God, I love You and pray that You open my eyes so I may see myself as You do. Open my ears so I may hear You clearly, and open my heart so I may receive and believe Your words wholeheartedly. Help me to become all You created me to be.

In the name of Christ Jesus, Redeemer of the destitute (downtrodden, brokenhearted), Lord Jehovah. Amen.

CHAPTER ONE

Get Past Your Past and On to Your Future

If you are dealing with insecurity, regret, or an inferiority complex, your answers to the following questions will help clarify where you are concerning your past and present. And believe it or not, your answers to these questions could even determine the possible course of your future.

1) Do you sometimes feel that you are not good enough? That you do not measure up to others (siblings, peers, etc.)?

2) Do you expect things to go wrong in your life?

3) Have past mistakes caused you to be too careful or cautious in life regarding relationships, investments, raising children, or stepping out of your comfort zone?

4) Have you ever accused someone of picking on you or putting you down because he or she pointed out something that you need to let go of or develop?

If you answered, "Yes, that's me" to even one of these questions, you are reading the right book!

We all need to face our insecurities, regrets, and inferiority complexes if we are ever going to move on to our future.

Your Belief System

Our thoughts are created by our beliefs that tell us how we feel and how to act or react in various situations or circumstances. Our belief system determines the position we take in a particular situation or circumstance and can be either positive or negative. In either case, how we view a situation or circumstance can have a profound impact on our present and future success.

What controls your mind/thought process controls you!

The Bible tells us that a house divided cannot stand (Matthew 12:25). In your house (your mind), you cannot be divided in your thinking if you want to be a success in life. If you are trying to do one thing but are thinking in another direction, you are destined to fail because your mind is divided.

The good thing about mistakes is that they let us know that we can do better, be better, and have better. We do not need to wallow in our mistakes or feel bad about them; instead, we can make them work for us. Mistakes can be useful, as they can help us assess what happened and learn what should have happened.

WHAT DOES "INFERIORITY" MEAN?

"Inferiority" is a feeling of being less than someone else, second-rate, inadequate.

People feel inferior when they measure themselves to standards they cannot meet such as a worldly standard, a peer standard, or a superstar standard. For example, the world's standard says the way to achieve happiness is to become rich and have lots of money. However, that is not the biblical standard. God's standard for being rich and happy is to have Jesus in your heart and live in obedience to His plan for your life.

Feeling inferior comes when you have some idea or standard you aspire to emulate (something or someone you want to copy or measure up to). Feeling inferior can be intensified by dysfunctional environmental factors, such as family, friends, television shows, and music that are not healthy.

WHAT IS AN INFERIORITY COMPLEX?

When a person's sense of being inadequate persists for some time, it can become an inferiority complex. People with an inferiority complex tend to put themselves down. Sometimes they overcompensate for their low opinion of themselves by being overly.

An inferiority complex can have many faces and is derived from many roots. But in every case, a person who feels extremely inferior about something—be it looks, speech, or intelligence—is thinking within a framework of comparison to another person or group. That comparison could be made in relation to the person's family or peer group, a superstar, a movie idol, etc. In all cases, people with inferiority complexes *fear* that they do not measure up to whatever person or group they are comparing themselves to.

Most of us do not want other people to see what we perceive as our weaknesses or what hurts us. But from a biblical view, God already sees our hurts, and He knows our weaknesses. He knows all about our problems, and He understands. As Matthew 8:17 says, "That it might be fulfilled which was spoken by Esaias the prophet, saying, Himself took our *infirmities*, and bare our sicknesses" (emphasis added). Jesus knows your infirmities and weaknesses, and He came to carry your burdens and to heal you.

Feelings of inferiority come from our doubts or inner fears that we are inadequate. Many of us are so messed up in our thinking that we sincerely believe we deserve to be punished or deserve to live in fear of punishment. Some even fear that "things are going so well that something has to happen to mess this up." That is called "fear of success."

But from a biblical perspective, God is not waiting for man to mess up or fail to live up to His high expectations. God already knows what we are capable of and that we have faults and failings. He asks only that we repent of our sins and then move on. (I will share more about His amazing grace in a later chapter.)

Unfortunately, we mistakenly believe that because we do not measure up to God's standards, He will not answer our prayers. We know He can, but we do not believe that He will. But the biblical view is that once we accept Jesus Christ into our lives and repent of our sins, we become righteous through His shed blood.

> *Confess your faults one to another, and pray one for another, that ye may be healed. The effectual fervent prayer of a righteous man availeth much.*
>
> (James 5:16, emphasis added)

The idea that one is inferior is often an unconscious feeling. Whether conscious or unconscious, the sense of inadequacy can propel people to actions that are not healthy or socially attractive. There are three basic behavioral patterns that individuals employ to try to compensate for their feelings of inferiority:

1) They seek societal approval.
2) They seek positive affirmation.
3) They seek constructive confirmation.

WHAT ABOUT REGRET?

These behaviors seldom produce the desired results (of making people feel better about themselves), so they end in regret. Regret is not the same as guilt; regret is disappointment, feeling sorry about what was done or left undone. Regrets are lingering, nagging thoughts about past mistakes.

People understand that when they make a decision, they will regret making the wrong one. As a result, many are reluctant to make any decisions at all; they fear their decisions will cause unpleasant results—results they may or may not have anticipated.

Sydney Smith, a prominent early nineteenth–century clergyman, pointed out that God designed us to succeed. But if we fail to make the decisions we need to make to become the success that God intended us to be, the consequences of our inaction will be far worse than if we had boldly made decisions.

An insecure (or uncertain) person lacks confidence in his or her self-worth or value, capabilities, and ability to make good decisions. Individuals conceal their insecurities in various ways. They may set up defense mechanisms or justify their inaction. For instance, someone who drinks excessively might be trying to cover up feelings of shyness and low self-esteem that stem from past rejection. By drinking, that person becomes the "life of the party" and thus temporarily overcomes his or her insecurity and shyness to mingle with the crowd.

MISTAKES AND DOUBTS

Feelings of inadequacy are often the result of self-doubt. Doubts come from inner fears that we mistakenly believe to be true. Of course, these fears that we are inferior are not true because Christ, by His death on the cross, redeemed us and made all of us more than adequate.

The world teaches that when we mess up or make mistakes, we will be punished. When we Christians accept that lie, we unintentionally downplay the true work of Christ—His redemption, forgiveness, and amazing grace (supernatural ability).

Many mistakenly believe that because of who they think they are or because of what they have done, trying to better themselves is not worth the effort because there is nothing they can do to change; they think they will always be the same old person. That is a lie from the pit of hell!

The simple truth is that when we have suffered and experienced pain, we have been proven by the fire. The trials (or fire) of life are what build and mold our character. So when we survive our trials, we learn that we can set our minds to become better people (by building our character).

Mistakes are normal parts of life; we all make them. The important thing is how we view our mistakes. Most importantly, how we react to them really matters.

Stay in your mistakes, and you will sink.
Learn from your mistakes and move on.
Your past does not determine your future.

CHAPTER TWO

Never Stop Trying

Insecurities need an avenue to work through, something to attach themselves to—a base of operation. Fear often serves as that vehicle. Insecurities manifest themselves through a thought process that is triggered by an event or an experience, such as a failed test or an overdue bill.

These insecurities are primary factors that hinder us from going forth and living productive, prosperous lives in Christ. Our insecurities inhibit us from becoming all that our Creator intended us to become.

Remember, virtually all the mighty men of the Bible failed in some task and were insecure about something. Moses felt obligated to point out to God that he was not a good speaker; Jeremiah protested that he was too young to serve as a prophet; David committed adultery, failed at fatherhood, and was a murderer, yet God called him a man after His own heart (1 Samuel 13:14); and Solomon was a womanizer.

My friend, insecurity and failure are not sins! The important point to grasp here is that failure is a temporary situation and cannot have a lasting impact upon your life unless you accept and embrace it.

God calls you to be faithful. That means you may fail in a task, but you do not have to let it get you down. Instead, stay faithful to the goal by trying as many times as it takes to get the assignment right.

**If you stop trying,
you will never succeed.**

You may be knocked down, but you can get back up and into the ring.

**It is not a disgrace to fail,
but it is a disgrace to give up.**

Alexander Graham Bell once said that when one door closes, another one opens. But he also pointed out that people tend to look at the closed door for so long and with so much regret that they miss seeing the open one! not see the ones which open for us.

A PERSONAL SHARING

When I first started getting my life together, I was insecure about many things. I had many regrets, and I felt inferior to others in countless ways. But God spoke to my heart and said, "If you just do your best, I'll do the rest." Success is determined by our efforts. In my case, I believe I got an A for putting forth my best effort.

God already knew whether I would fail or not. In any task at hand, I therefore tried to succeed. Even if I failed, there was always a lesson to be learned. So I tried to learn those lessons and grow.

Let go of the issues and failures of your past, as they will cause you to hesitate to possess your future. Let go and become all that God has created and intended you to be.

The past will not let you go unless you let it go.

As long as you hold on to the past by reasoning, justifying, or excusing your failures, you will always be stuck in old potholes. Don't stay stuck by saying, "I can't do this because . . . ," "I am like this because . . . ," or "He said that to me, and I've never been the same."

CHAPTER THREE

Steps to Freedom from Insecurities

The first step toward freedom is to *identify your insecurities*. Ask yourself:

- What keeps me from being all I was created to be?
- What keeps me from totally trusting God with my life?
- Who or what intimidates me?

Then, ask yourself, "Why do I think the way I do?" Is it because of childhood trauma? Childhood trauma can come from extensive teasing; physical, emotional, or alcohol and drug abuse in the home; or constant criticism from others. Perhaps you were told, "Why should you try that? You've failed at everything else."

Once you have identified your insecurities, the next step is to *confess your insecurities before God*. You can then confront your insecurities directly, telling them,

"You no longer have dominion over me. You no longer have free rein in my life. I am under the blood of Jesus Christ, and I am forgiven."

A vital key to freedom from the past is *forgiveness*. You must let go of your past pain and any abuse from others. If you fail to let go, you will stay in bondage to the people and the hurts of the past. And you must even forgive yourself. To help in this area, read Psalm 91:1-16:

> *He that dwelleth in the secret place of the*
> *most High shall abide under the shadow of*
> *the Almighty.*
> *I will say of the lord, He is my refuge and*
> *my fortress: my God; in him will I trust.*
> *Surely he shall deliver thee from the*
> *snare of the fowler, and from the noisome*
> *pestilence.*
> *He shall cover thee with his feathers, and*
> *under his wings shalt thou trust: his truth*
> *shall be thy shield and buckler.*
> *Thou shalt not be afraid for the terror by*
> *night; nor for the arrow that flieth by day;*
> *Nor for the pestilence that walketh in*
> *darkness; nor for the destruction that*
> *wasteth at noonday.*
> *A thousand shall fall at thy side, and ten*
> *thousand at thy right hand; but it shall not*
> *come nigh thee.*

Only with thine eyes shalt thou behold and
see the reward of the wicked.
Because thou hast made the lord, which
is my refuge, even the most High, thy
habitation;
There shall no evil befall thee, neither shall
any plague come nigh thy dwelling.
For he shall give his angels charge over thee,
to keep thee in all thy ways.
They shall bear thee up in their hands, lest
thou dash thy foot against a stone.
Thou shalt tread upon the lion and adder:
the young lion and the dragon shalt thou
trample under feet.
Because he hath set his love upon me,
therefore will I deliver him: I will set him on
high, because he hath known my name.
He shall call upon me, and I will answer
him: I will be with him in trouble; I will
deliver him, and honour him.
With long life will I satisfy him, and shew
him my salvation.

Claim these promises in Psalm 91 for your own life. Declare passionately, "I receive the promises of God because I am a new creation in Christ. God will not withhold any good thing from me. I am free!"

God loves you so much! Even if your earthly father has been a great blessing in your life, God is far greater than your earthly father could possibly be. And if your earthly father or someone else has hurt you, allow God to heal your hurts and to show you your true worth. You are important to God.

Know that there is a place of security in Christ alone, as the following Scripture illustrates:

> *And hath raised us up together, and made us sit together in heavenly places in Christ Jesus . . . For we are his workmanship, created in Christ Jesus unto good works, which God hath before ordained that we should walk in them (Ephesians 2:6, 10).*

CHAPTER FOUR

On Becoming a New Creature

As you read this book, let go of those past hurts, failures, and negative experiences, thoughts, and decisions. As 2 Corinthians 5:17 says, "Therefore if any man be in Christ, he is a new creature: old things are passed away; behold, all things are become new." What the devil meant for harm in your life (sin), God has turned around (your old life) for the good!

The truth is: we are always drawn in two directions at the same time: (1) toward the flesh, which is affected by our problems, or (2) toward the Spirit of God, which is not affected by our problems. In each situation one has to lead—the flesh or the Spirit; they cannot both lead in the same situation.

The children of Israel provide an example of being drawn in two directions. When they left Egypt and before they entered the Promised Land, they had one major problem: They could not let go of their flesh, and that is what led them:

> *And they took their journey from Elim, and all the congregation of the children of Israel came unto the wilderness of Sin, which is between Elim and Sinai, on the fifteenth day of the second month after their departing out of the land of Egypt. And the whole congregation of the children of Israel murmured against Moses and Aaron in the wilderness: And the children of Israel said unto them, Would to God we had died by the hand of the Lord in the land of Egypt, when we sat by the flesh pots, and when we did eat bread to the full; for ye have brought us forth into this wilderness, to kill this whole assembly with hunger (Exodus 16:1-3).*

The wilderness in this passage essentially represents the flesh, illustrated by hunger and fasting. The Israelites needed to kill their flesh before they could enter into the Promised Land. And like the Israelites, we need to let go of our flesh before we can enter our Promised Land.

In the Israelites' journey to the Promised Land, God gave them a time of sanctification and a place where they could get to know God, to trust His provision, to learn to follow Him (the cloud and the fire), and to learn to worship Him in spirit and in truth.

> *Then said the Lord unto Moses, Behold, I will rain bread from heaven for you; and the people shall go out and gather a certain rate every day, that I may prove them, whether they will walk in my law, or no (Exodus 16:4).*

The Israelites did not understand, nor did they see the benefits of the wilderness compared to the place they had left (Egypt). They relied on their flesh—their old, familiar thoughts and patterns of behavior—to determine where they wanted to go. Our past is our wilderness, the place where we need to consecrate ourselves unto the Lord.

The Israelites failed to kill their flesh but instead chose to follow it (their selfish desires) by murmuring and complaining about their hunger, their thirst, and about wanting to die or return to Egypt. They focused on what they had left in Egypt, not on the abundance of the Promised Land where God had already made provision for them.

God does not see the problems in your life;
He sees only your faith!

God already knows your needs and desires, and they are not problems for Him. He wants you to see those needs and desires as opportunities for your faith to work, transforming you into the person He wants you to be—one who entirely trusts and depends upon Him.

IMPROVE THE QUALITY OF YOUR LIFE

Something or someone always influences us in life. But how much we allow circumstances or people to impact the quality of our lives is determined by the way we see and respond to them. Our responses can be affected (either consciously or subconsciously) by past experiences that are similar to our present circumstances.

When the prodigal son returned home, his father put his best robe on him (Jesus is the robe of righteousness). He also put a ring (a seal) on his son's finger, which represented their union. (The Holy Spirit is our seal.) Like the prodigal son's father, who gave his love and forgiveness instantly to his wayward child, God loves you. Despite your past, when you return to Him, He accepts you based not upon your goodness or righteousness, but on God's righteousness.

Let the Word of God transform your mind; do not let your experiences in life corrupt or distort the message of His Word. Move beyond the veils of human reasoning, self-satisfaction, and old patterns to embrace positive affirmations for healing, blessing, and strength. Refuse to wallow in negative affirmations that re-open your wounds and slow down your healing. Negativity poisons your mind and thus pulls down the quality of your life.

Move away from the harmful events brought about by wrong thinking.

Allow God to mold you into His image. As Isaiah 64:8 says, "But now, O Lord, thou art our father; we are the clay, and thou our potter; and we all are the work of thy hand." He uses your life situations to shape you to look like Him, developing your dependence on Him as you build character by allowing Him to work within you and transform your thinking.

CHAPTER FIVE

The Enemy Is Still Working

Satan never accepts defeat. He never stops trying to mold us into his likeness, trying to get us to see things his way through events, people, and worldly desires. He is your enemy who wants you to dwell on and wallow in your past failures until you feel ugly, unworthy, and inferior.

But past failures do not affect God. He has cast our sins and all of our past into a sea of forgetfulness. He has placed our faults and sins under the blood of Jesus, and the devil cannot bring them back.

> *Repent ye therefore, and be converted, that your sins may be blotted out, when the times of refreshing shall come from the presence of the Lord.*
>
> (Acts 3:19)

> *For as the heaven is high above the earth, so*
> *great is his mercy toward them that fear him.*
> *As far as the east is from the west, so far hath*
> *he removed our transgressions from us.*
>
> (Psalm 103:11-12)

If God is willing to forget about your past and your sins, why do you allow the devil or anyone else to accuse you before Him or bring your failings back up? God will never place you back into the bondage of your past sins or failures because doing so would make His sacrifice on the cross of no value.

> *He hath not dealt with us after our sins; nor*
> *rewarded us according to our iniquities.*
>
> (Psalm 103:10)

> *I, even I, am he that blotteth out thy*
> *transgressions for mine own sake, and will*
> *not remember thy sins.*
>
> (Isaiah 43:25)

The enemy will try to use your past to bring you into condemnation, and he will accuse you. His greatest weapon is to get you to agree with the lies he is feeding you. Focus your thoughts on the words of Paul:

> *There is therefore now no condemnation to*
> *them which are in Christ Jesus, who walk not*

after the flesh, but after the Spirit. For the law of the Spirit of life in Christ Jesus hath made me free from the law of sin and death. For what the law could not do, in that it was weak through the flesh, God sending his own Son in the likeness of sinful flesh, and for sin, condemned sin in the flesh. (Romans 8:1-3).

Your past failures do not determine your future!

How you see things in the present and how you handle your life (obeying good instruction) is what God is looking for. The primary determinants to being a child of God are your standing with Him and your obedience to His Word.

Amazingly, the blood of Christ even covers your present failures!

For we have not an high priest which cannot be touched with the feeling of our infirmities; but was in all points tempted like as we are, yet without sin. Let us therefore come boldly unto the throne of grace, that we may obtain mercy, and find grace to help in time of need.

(Hebrews 4:15-16)

CHAPTER SIX

Do You See Giants?

And they went and came to Moses, and to Aaron, and to all the congregation of the children of Israel, unto the wilderness of Paran, to Kadesh; and brought back word unto them, and unto all the congregation, and shewed them the fruit of the land. And they told him, and said, We came unto the land whither thou sentest us, and surely it floweth with milk and honey; and this is the fruit of it. Nevertheless the people be strong that dwell in the land, and the cities are walled, and very great: and moreover, we saw the children of Anak there. The Amalekites dwell in the land of the south: and the Hittites, and the Jebusites, and the Amorites, dwell in the mountains: and the Canaanites dwell by the sea, and by the coast of Jordan. And Caleb stilled the people before Moses, and said, Let us go up at once, and possess it; for we are well able to overcome it. But the men that went up with him said, We be not able to go up against the people; for they are stronger than we. And they brought up an evil report of the land which they had searched unto the children of Israel, saying, The land, through which we have gone to search it, is a land that eateth up the inhabitants thereof; and all the people that we saw in it are men of a great stature. And there we saw the giants, the sons of Anak, which come of the giants: and we were in our own sight as grasshoppers, and so we were in their sight.

(Numbers 13:26-33)

In this passage, twelve Israelites spent forty days spying out the land of Canaan, seeking some assurance of success as they ventured forth into the Promised Land, a gift from God Almighty. However, ten of the spies had doubts about God's power and promise based upon what they saw—mighty giants and great walls. They saw their circumstances through eyes with limited ability to perceive accurately (their thought process).

But Joshua and Caleb were dramatically different. Although they saw the same things as the ten, they based their confidence in the success of the conquest of the land on God's abilities, not their own. These men were secure in God's love and ability. They did not just believe in Him, but they passionately believed that their God was more than enough! How we think affects our actions: "For as he thinketh in his heart, so is he" (Proverbs 23:7).

TOUGH QUESTION, REAL ANSWER

You may ask, "Why do unjust things happen to people who have not done anything to deserve it?" Others might ask, "Why was I born into a dysfunctional family?" or "Why did my father abuse me?" or "Why did my parents abandon me?"

We know that God is the author of all that is good and perfect; therefore, we know, by process of elimination, that it is not God's will for these painful events to happen in our lives. We also know that the fall of man, succumbing to Satan's temptation, brought evil into this world, and that Satan is responsible for virtually all evil.

I know this is a brief explanation, and it may not do the subject justice or comfort you in extreme pain. I ask only that you keep in mind that no matter how painful your circumstances have been or are now, *God has provided a way out*! He desires you to experience peace and prosperity in your life.

Another attempt to answer this tough question is that God created the laws of nature, including reaping and sowing, day and night, the seasons, and free will.

He created the systems, and He honors those systems. He intervenes only when one of His children asks Him to and when the request is in accordance with His will, which is always good. There are times when God allows things to come upon humankind to encourage man to turn to Him for protection, guidance, and love.

Learn to depend upon Him and His goodness. Give Him the glory that He deserves. Apart from Him, we are helpless!

> *And God saw everything that he had made, and, behold, it was very good. And the evening and the morning were the sixth day.*
>
> (Genesis 1:31, emphasis added).

God the Father will never do you any harm!

I know that I would never intentionally harm my children. And I will protect them from ugly circumstances as long as avoiding those circumstances is good for them. If you want to see me really upset, just try to mess with one of my children!

If we as parents love our children this much, how much more does God love us? Remember, He always gives His best for us.

Joseph Had to Get Over It!

Joseph had to get over what his brothers did to him in order to move on to his future.

> *But as for you, ye thought evil against me;*
> *but God meant it unto good, to bring to pass,*
> *as it is this day, to save much people alive.*
> (Genesis 50:20)

Joseph did not allow what his brothers did to him to dictate the direction of his life. He trusted God and knew that He was ultimately in control of his destiny. Therefore, he had no regrets. He was not insecure, and he did not feel inferior to anyone. His attitude was echoed by Paul:

> Brethren, I count not myself to have apprehended: but this one thing I do, *forgetting those things which are behind*, and reaching forth unto those things which are before, I press toward the mark for the prize of the high calling of God in Christ Jesus.
> (Philippians 3:13-14, emphasis added)

> *There hath no temptation taken you but such as is common to man: but God is faithful, who will not suffer you to be tempted above that ye are able; but will with the temptation*

also make a way to escape, that ye may be
able to bear it.

(1 Corinthians 10:13)

Joseph understood God's Word to be true, and his life was a strong witness to that fact. His attitude is one we should emulate and embrace.

CHAPTER SEVEN

Monitoring the Mind

The problem is that most of the time our minds are already made up before we have all the facts. Then, when we get new information, the new facts are piled upon other facts, and conclusion may change. God's truths, however, never change; they are absolute.

Human beings take things at face value, based upon how they perceive what they experience (until they learn to think differently). Our five senses of touch, taste, sight, hearing, and smell play pivotal roles in creating and reinforcing our belief systems. Some of our experiences offer good initial sensations but then have a negative impact, such as taking drugs, drinking alcohol, and having multiple sexual partners. Many types of experiences, especially in excess, are not good for us, but we mistakenly believe that the momentary pleasure of these destructive activities outweighs their negative effects.

Whatever our deceptions, they can be exposed only by biblical truths, line upon line, precept upon precept. Alcoholics may truly believe that drinking is good because it makes them feel better, but after objectively analyzing the devastating results of alcohol upon their lives, they can begin to see a new truth about drinking.

Perception is the process by which we gain immediate awareness of what is happening outside of our experiential senses. For example, even though we see with our eyes, our vision is limited. We can see only one of the more than sixty octaves of radiation light emitted by the sun. But when we are tuned into the spirit world, a realm outside the physical dimension experienced through the senses, our perception can be enhanced.

Because of the limitations of our physical senses, our minds are limited in how they interpret our experiences. Our minds understand natural phenomena and experiences more simply than they actually are. In essence, the mind has a "perceptual prejudice" based upon the easiest way to interpret something.

For example, two rows of corn may appear to meet at some point in the distance, but they never actually do. The limitations of the eye simply do not allow you to see the rows of corn as they really are. Also, the moon appears larger at the horizon than it does when at mid-sky. But the size of the moon itself never changes. These simple examples demonstrate that perceptions of reality based solely on our five senses fails to produce pure truth.

Perceived truth is reinforced by our senses and is modified by our past and present experiences.

A REASON TO CHANGE

For people to change, they need to have a motivation, a reason to make think or act differently. If the reason to remain the same outweighs the reason to change, people will more than likely remain the same or keep doing what they have been doing—even if it has a detrimental outcome.

If you plan to move on to your future, you have to stop dwelling on your past memories and failures. You need to modify your thinking, your imagination, and your vision by developing a plan of action. Now, that does not mean you will totally forget your past experiences, but rather it means you will learn from them and *then* let them go.

Do not let your past memories and experiences dictate your future!

What you believe will ultimately determine what you say and do and will impact whether you arrive at your targeted destination.

Plato's Cave

In Plato's "The Allegory of the Cave," he presented an extended metaphor contrasting the way we perceive reality with what we believe is reality. He demonstrated that we all perceive imperfect "reflections" of truth and reality.

In Plato's fictional cave, prisoners are chained down and forced to look only at the front wall of the cave. They are unable to turn their heads and view what is going on behind them. Behind them are puppeteers who are casting shadows on the wall, and the prisoners perceive the shadows as reality.

Plato's allegory demonstrates how difficult it is for humans to make realistic, valid conclusions based solely upon their senses. The prisoners could see only the wall of the cave, yet behind them burned a fire that provided light whereby the puppeteers cast shadows on the wall of the cave. When the prisoners saw the shadows and heard the echoes of objects they did not see, they mistook the shadows and echoes for reality. This allegory aptly demonstrates how *reality can be manipulated.*

Circumstances can manipulate our perception of reality, just as much as if we were chained in a cave. How we were trained, the reactions we learned, and how and where we were raised all determine how we will respond to an event.

What we believe to be true becomes our belief system. "Since it is true for me, it must be true for others."

Another Cave Perspective

As effective as Plato's illustration is, it does not take into account that all reality can be exposed to the truth (the light) that brings clarity. The issue is embracing the *proper* light (truth). In the process of time, as the light (truth of God) becomes engrafted in individuals, it enables them to see clearly beyond their circumstances.

CHAPTER EIGHT

Reflecting on and Refuting Insecurity and Regrets

First Kings 19:1-2, 4 presents yet another story related to insecurity, regrets, and feelings of inferiority:

> *And Ahab told Jezebel all that Elijah had done, and withal how he had slain all the prophets with the sword. Then Jezebel sent a messenger unto Elijah, saying, So let the gods do to me, and more also, if I make not thy life as the life of one of them by to-morrow about this time . . . But he himself went a day's journey into the wilderness, and came and sat down under a juniper tree: and he requested for himself that he might die; and said, It is enough; now, O Lord, take away my life; for I am not better than my fathers.*

Elijah was a mighty man of God, but when he received the message from Jezebel, and based upon what he saw (the picture he had formed in his mind), he became distressed, left town, and wished he could die. He even asked God to take his life!

Deep down, Elijah's actions indicate that he was really insecure about God's power and ability to deliver on what He had promised. Elijah had just come down from Mount Carmel, and God had showed Himself strong, giving Elijah victory in 1 Kings 18.

But Elijah had given power to the words of a wicked woman by believing what she said, allowing her words to dishearten him, and then seeing himself as inferior. What Elijah was really saying to himself was that God was not capable; God was not adequate in His ability to protect him.

Because of that false truth, Elijah ran away (about two hundred miles in total) to the desert and entered a cave, a place of darkness. Both the desert and the cave represent dejection; Elijah's unfounded insecurity (his fear for his life) drove him where he did not have to go. He was wallowing in self-pity, the "poor me" syndrome, and felt all alone. Elijah allowed his fear to lead him into depression and distress.

"What Are You Doing Here?"

> *And he said, Go forth, and stand upon the*
> *mount before the Lord. And, behold, the*

> *Lord passed by, and a great and strong wind*
> *rent the mountains, and brake in pieces the*
> *rocks before the Lord; but the Lord was not in*
> *the wind: and after the wind an earthquake;*
> *but the Lord was not in the earthquake: And*
> *after the earthquake a fire; but the Lord was*
> *not in the fire: and after the fire a still small*
> *voice. And it was so, when Elijah heard it that*
> *he wrapped his face in his mantle, and went*
> *out, and stood in the entering in of the cave.*
> *And, behold, there came a voice unto him,*
> *and said, What doest thou here, Elijah?*
>
> (1 Kings 19:11-13)

The first question God put to Elijah was essentially, "Elijah, what are you doing here?" That is the same question we should all ask ourselves when we are faced with fear: "What am I doing here? Am I where I should be?"

The good news is that God was and still is on the throne. He was able to meet Elijah wherever he was, and He will meet us where we are.

Although Elijah was in the wrong place, God, without speaking, caused a strong wind to break up the rock (just as Elijah was broken), and then, again without speaking, He caused an earthquake (symbolic of Elijah's shaken faith). Next, without speaking, God caused fire (as Elijah was being purged by the spiritual fire that consumes and cleans). Finally, God spoke to Elijah in a still, small voice (a place of peace).

Understand this: As long as Elijah was consumed with his thoughts and distracted by all the commotion, he could not hear the voice of God. The way we hear God's voice is to settle down and get rid of our distractions (the past and our self-pity) so that we might hear God's instructions as to what to do next.

Elijah ran to Mount Horeb, "the mountain of the true God," the same place where Moses had received his commission (the place of the burning bush in Exodus 3:1) and where Israel received the Ten Commandments from God through Moses.

Moses too had insecurities from his past experiences, insecurities that caused him to actually debate with God as to whether he was the right man for the job:

> *Who am I, that I should go unto Pharaoh . . . What shall I say unto them? . . . But, behold, they will not believe me, nor hearken unto my voice . . . I am not eloquent, neither heretofore, nor since thou hast spoken unto thy servant: but I am slow of speech, and of a slow tongue.*
>
> (Exodus 3:11, 13; 4:1, 10)

Anything that exalts itself over the knowledge of God, the only truth, makes itself to be "as God" in your life.

Moreover, anything contrary to the Word of God is only a provisional presupposition because God is omniscient (all-knowing) and He deals only with certainties, the absolute realities. Man deals with possibilities, measuring and evaluating them based upon perceptions of grandeur.

Abandon Your Worldview

Anything contrary to what God thinks about you or your circumstances is based upon a lie!

How you perceive an event or understand your position is not necessarily an accurate picture of your circumstances. For example, dirt is comprised of the same minerals as the human body in about the same proportions, yet when you look at the ground you see dirt, but when you look at a human, you see a living, breathing being bearing the very image of God!

CHAPTER NINE

Forgive and Learn from Your Past

Do not ever forget what you have been through. To get beyond your past, you must let go of all the hurt and the pains, but you must learn from the memories, especially the painful ones, and then move forward. The past was then, and now is now.

To experience closure from your past, you must be willing to forgive others as well as yourself. When a judge closes a court case, he will not re-open it except for a highly significant reason.

In the court of heaven, when God closes your case, the only one who can re-open it is *you*. That is why I always tell the enemy (my thoughts, the devil, etc.), when he tries to force me to re-open my past, to "hang it on the cross" because that is where the case remains—dealt with, closed, and buried forever.

Forgiveness is an important part of letting go and moving on. You have to forgive even when you feel you cannot forgive. Forgiveness does not let the perpetrator off the hook; it frees you from the pain of reliving the hurt. As you experience forgiveness, you can even eventually grow to love the perpetrator through Christ's love. You can learn to view the negative experiences instigated by Satan as the past—over and done with—and begin to thank Jesus for His death on the cross for your sins. Remember, He died for you in spite of your failings and sins.

FORGIVENESS IS PERSONAL

I praise and thank God for His goodness. There have been so many times in my life when I knew God was calling and wooing me to come to Him but I kept rejecting Him. Even the apostle Paul had major sins and offenses, yet he was the one God selected to write the majority of the New Testament. He had to get over his past. And he learned from it.

Paul remained humble because of what he had done in the past. His own failings helped him to stay humble and to understand the faults and sins of others.

> *And lest I should be exalted above measure through the abundance of the revelations, there was given to me a thorn in the flesh, the messenger of Satan to buffet me, lest I should be exalted above measure. For this thing I*

> *besought the Lord thrice, that it might depart*
> *from me. And he said unto me, My grace is*
> *sufficient for thee: for my strength is made*
> *perfect in weakness. Most gladly therefore*
> *will I rather glory in my infirmities, that the*
> *power of Christ may rest upon me. Therefore*
> *I take pleasure in infirmities, in reproaches,*
> *in necessities, in persecutions, in distresses*
> *for Christ's sake: for when I am weak, then*
> *am I strong.*

(2 Corinthians 12:7-10)

Some believe Paul was writing about some type of bodily affliction (ulcer, poor eyes, etc.), and that may be the case. But I believe it is possible that Paul was saying that a messenger of Satan was sent to remind him of what and who he was—a killer of Christians.

Today, Satan's messengers are still trying to remind us of our faults. Whatever the case, you can count on one thing: Satan and his messengers tried to get Paul to focus on his past in order to diminish his present and future impact on the body of Christ.

What Does "Die to Flesh" Mean?

> *What shall we say then? Shall we continue*
> *in sin, that grace may abound? God forbid.*
> *How shall we, that are dead to sin, live any*
> *longer therein? Know ye not, that so many of*

us as were baptized into Jesus Christ were baptized into his death? Therefore we are buried with him by baptism into death: that like as Christ was raised up from the dead by the glory of the Father, even so we also should walk in newness of life. For if we have been planted together in the likeness of his death, we shall be also in the likeness of his resurrection: Knowing this, that our old man is crucified with him, that the body of sin might be destroyed, that henceforth we should not serve sin. For he that is dead is freed from sin. Now if we be dead with Christ, we believe that we shall also live with him: Knowing that Christ being raised from the dead dieth no more; death hath no more dominion over him. For in that he died, he died unto sin once: but in that he liveth, he liveth unto God. Likewise reckon ye also yourselves to be dead indeed unto sin, but alive unto God through Jesus Christ our Lord. Let not sin therefore reign in your mortal body, that ye should obey it in the lusts thereof. Neither yield ye your members as instruments of unrighteousness unto sin: but yield yourselves unto God, as those that are alive from the dead, and your members as instruments of righteousness unto God.

> *For sin shall not have dominion over you: for*
> *ye are not under the law, but under grace.*
> (Romans 6:1-14)

This passage begins by explaining that God forbids us from continuing to sin. It states that His grace (the goodness of God) will grow and increase in us, freeing us as we learn to "die to flesh." That phrase means that as we allow God's grace to free us from sin, we kill the "flesh" (sinful nature) in us, freeing ourselves from past, present, and future bondage. As the flesh dies, we grow to live in the Spirit, which means we put away our old habits and stop doing things that please the flesh.

No matter how hard it may seem to give up drugs, alcohol, sexual sins, or any other bondage, when we "die to the flesh" and begin living under God's grace, we live a life that is not ruled by our circumstances. We will seek out that which is good and live according to the Word of God, which presents God's standards rather than worldly or fleshly desires. The things that seem right or pleasurable to man are not the standards we are to follow. When we live unto the Lord, we die to self and its desires.

The more we live for God, the more we die to our self—our past thoughts; our emotions; and the old, unregenerate self. Our lives become about pleasing Him more than pleasing ourselves (even if it hurts at first) because we know that in the long run pleasing Him is the best thing for us.

This transformation process in which we die to self enables us to stop sin from ruling over us (verses 13-14) as we surrender to God. And once we are surrendered to God, even though we do not have to obey the law, we are so transformed that we will not do anything but obey God's laws.

CHAPTER TEN

The War of Words

We are always at war with our thoughts (flesh). That is why we allow the Holy Spirit to kill our flesh so that we can bring every thought captive to the truth that Jesus has set us free from hurts, troubles, heartaches, and sins and has given us dominion over these things.

There are times when Satan brings back to my mind the hurts I have caused others and the hurts I suffered from others. Sometimes he tries to accuse me of neglecting my children and reminds me, "Things would be a lot better for you now if you hadn't made so many bad decisions." When these thoughts enter my mind, I rebuke them in the name of Jesus. Although they may still echo in my mind, through the power of Jesus I no longer allow them to have dominion over me.

Early in my rededication to God, I had some fears and temptations from my past. But gradually God gave me a deep relationship with Him and victory over my past. When I first got back into relationship with Him, honestly, I was still afraid of falling back into patterns of my past. He told me, "You do your best, and I'll do the rest." He then said, "The only way you can fail, even if you fall, is if you do not get back up and try again."

LIFE IS LIKE SCHOOL

If you fail a test, you brush yourself off, study some more, and take the test again until you pass. The struggle only makes you better, not bitter.

You see, God already knows everything that has happened or will ever happen. He already knows about your past, your present, and your future—good and bad—and He loves you anyway.

As far as your past is concerned, it will stay in the past as long as you leave it there and let it go. *Let go of your past and it will let go of you.* Deal with it, and move on. You are destined for better things.

At times, I still need to remind myself that my past abuses are just that—in my past. I do regret how I wasted time pursuing my desires rather than God's desires for me. Frankly, I lost a lot of time. I regret not being the type of father I should have been to my children. I have three children by three different women; as a result, I was not in their lives as I should have been. Thankfully, today I have good relationships with all my children.

But to have a productive present, I had to move on from my feelings of guilt, regret, and pride, all the while keeping in mind that God was and is determined to love me in spite of my past and present shortcomings.

God loves you in spite of yourself. He sees the good in you, and if you allow Him to work in you to come into agreement with what He thinks about you and how He sees you, the negative things that once had dominion and authority over you will no longer remain the focal point of your life.

The Bible declares that we have nothing to be afraid of or anxious about if we keep our minds focused on Him. "Thou wilt keep him in perfect peace, whose mind is stayed on thee: *because he trusteth in thee*" (Isaiah 26:3, emphasis added).

God plans only what is good for your future, but what you do, think, or say can further or hinder the future God plans for you. For example, if a man drinks alcohol excessively, eventually he may contract liver disease. Now, it was not in God's plan for this man to develop the disease; it was the man's drinking that caused the disease.

You cannot change your past, but you can change your future!

Start today releasing all of your insecurities, letting go of all your regrets, and liberating yourself from your inferiority complex.

You are somebody to God. He has His mind on you, thinks about you night and day, and spreads His loving wings around you because you are special to Him.

> *I will praise thee; for I am fearfully and wonderfully made: marvellous are thy works; and that my soul knoweth right well.*
>
> (Psalm 139:14)

> *He that spared not his own Son, but delivered him up for us all, how shall he not with him also freely give us all things? Who shall lay anything to the charge of God's elect? It is God that justifieth.*
>
> (Romans 8:32-33)

Who shall accuse you? Shall it be your conscience? The devil and his demons? Shall it be your past? Your emotions? Others? God has justified, delivered, forgiven, strengthened, and set you free!

> *Who shall separate us from the love of Christ? shall tribulation, or distress, or persecution, or famine, or nakedness, or peril, or sword? . . . Nay, in all these things we are more than conquerors through him that loved us.*
>
> (Romans 8:35, 37)

Who or what are you going to allow to dictate to you who you are or what you can be or have? Who or what are you going to allow to separate you from your destiny?

Do not allow your regrets, insecurities, or inferior mind-set to condemn you. What is past is over, and your future is much brighter because you are more than a conqueror through Christ Jesus! Trust in God, who is the source, strength, and sanctity of your salvation. "And such trust have we through Christ to God-ward: Not that we are sufficient of ourselves to think any thing as of ourselves; but our sufficiency is of God" (2 Corinthians 3:4-5).

God is in you, and He is the source, the secret, the sanctuary, the sanctification, and the success of your power. Therefore, whatever comes your way, give it to Him and rejoice in the hope you have in Him and in His ability to heal, deliver, give peace, bring prosperity, and manifest your purpose.

> *And he said unto me, My grace is sufficient for thee: for my strength is made perfect in weakness. Most gladly therefore will I rather glory in my infirmities, that the power of Christ may rest upon me. Therefore I take pleasure in infirmities, in reproaches, in necessities, in persecutions, in d.istresses for Christ's sake: for when I am weak, then am I strong.*
>
> (2 Corinthians 12:9-10)

Do you see it? We are liberated from past hurts and failures. As we depend upon Him and embrace His Word, He will soothe, strengthen, reassure, and comfort our hearts. God will hold us in His arms, and He wants us to experience the freedom He brings. "Now the Lord is that Spirit: and where the Spirit of the Lord is, there is liberty" (2 Corinthians 3:17).

Do you have liberty over your past? Remember, your past has only the amount of rule, power, and control over your life that you give it. Rest in the Lord and in the power of His might. Be all that He has called you to be.

You can be a mighty man or woman of God!

Pray each of the following prayers until they become part of your heart.

Prayer for Forgiveness

Father God, Jehovah Tsidkenu (The lord Our Righteousness), I ask forgiveness for any unconfessed sins in my life, and I forgive those who have hurt me in any form, fashion, or way. Also, I release myself from any bitterness, wrong attitudes, and hatred. I release anything linked to unforgiveness in my heart.

Right now, I release others and myself from any word spoken by me or to me that I have been holding above forgiveness and deliverance. I release anything that is not of You and anything that is not representative of the love You have imparted to me.

Father, I receive now Your forgiveness, mercy, and grace. I welcome Your love for me and thank You for what Jesus did on the cross for me. Furthermore, I believe I have been forgiven and set free from insecurities, regrets, and the inferiority complex that once had me bound, unsure of who You created me to be and hesitant to walk in victory.

You are wonderful, my Balm of Gilead (Jeremiah 8:22), the Bishop of my soul (1 Peter 2:25). I surrender all of myself to You to have and to hold. In sickness and in health, I promise to serve You for the rest of my life.

Lord, I am hungry for You and ask You to create a clean heart in me and free me from of anything that offends You. In the name of Jesus, my Lord and Savior. Amen.

Prayer for Deliverance and Freedom

Father God, my redeemer, redemption, and refuge, I loose myself from double-mindedness, doubt, and unbelief and declare that I have been redeemed, reconciled, and restored from the injustices of my past. I am no longer bound to anger, strife, division, loneliness, and low self-esteem. Hebrews 8:12 declares that You will be merciful to my unrighteousness, and my sins and iniquities You will remember no more. Moreover, seeing that I am encompassed about with so great a cloud of witnesses, I lay aside every weight and the sin which doth so easily beset me, and will run with patience the race that is set before me (Hebrews 12:1). For He whom the Lord has made free is free indeed (John 8:36)! I am free! I am free! I am free! Amen.

Prayer to Give Up the Past

Father God, Jehovah Mekaddishkem (Lord our Sanctifier), You have not dealt with us after our sins, nor have you rewarded us according to our iniquities. For as the heaven is high above the earth, so great is Your mercy toward them that fear You, and as far as the east is from the west, hath You removed our transgressions from us (Psalm 103:10-12).

Therefore, in agreement with Isaiah 43:18-19, I will not keep in mind the former things, nor will I dwell upon or give regard or power to the things of my past. Father, You are doing a new thing in me; now it shall spring forth, and I shall see it, know it, and walk in it. Oh great God Almighty, thank You that You have made a way in the wilderness and rivers in the desert as a clear path for me to walk.

Because I am a new creation in Christ Jesus my Lord, old things are passed away; behold, all things are become new (2 Corinthians 5:17). Therefore, "I will praise thee, for I am fearfully and wonderfully made: marvellous are thy works; and that my soul knoweth right well" (Psalm 139:14). Amen.

Prayer to Die to Self and Live in Him

Father God, Elohim (God), You are the one and only true God. You are wonderful, marvelous, and mighty. In agreement with Romans 12:1-2, I present myself by Your mercies: my mind, body, and soul as "a living sacrifice, holy, acceptable unto God," which is the reasonable, sensible, sound, and intelligent thing that I can do as my act of service toward You.

In addition, I will not be conformed to this world. I release myself from worldly thoughts, attitudes, and desires. Furthermore, I commit myself to being transformed by the renewing of my mind, that I may prove what is Your good, acceptable, and perfect (complete) will, O God. Amen.

Prayer of Dedication to Him

Great God, Holy God, Adonai, Lord and Master, I give my whole heart to You and will learn of Your statutes. Write them upon the tablets of my heart, O Lord, that I might not transgress against You, nor regard illegitimate thoughts in mind or deceit or iniquity in my heart as I walk after Your ways, Your Word, and Your will in spirit and in truth.

Thank You that according to Romans 8:1 there is now no condemnation to me because I am in Christ Jesus, and so now I walk not after the flesh but after the Spirit of truth.

I reject and release all condemning, depressing spirits of despair *now*, for You, O God Jehovah Shalom (The lord our Peace), give me peace, and I rest in You. Amen.

Prayer Against Fear

Father God, Thy throne is forever and ever. Great is Your love toward me. I thank You that I have taken on the mind of Your Son, Jesus, and receive Your love in my heart.

Jeremiah 31:3 tells me that You, O Lord, "hath appeared of old unto me, saying, Yea, I have loved thee with an everlasting love: therefore with lovingkindness have I drawn thee." I am so grateful as I thank thee.

I loose myself from all fear because of the love You have for me. 1 John 4:18 demonstrates that "there is no fear in love; but perfect love casteth out fear: because fear hath torment."

Lord, I have peace because I trust in Thee. Therefore, in harmony with Proverbs 4:23, I keep my heart with all carefulness, "for out of it are the issues of life." And as Proverbs 23:7 states, "As [a man] thinketh in his heart, so is he."

I declare and decree that I am all You envisioned me to be, and I have no fear! Amen.

Prayer to Praise God

Emmanuel, Jehovah God, Advocate, Intercessor, Deliverer, Rock, Fortress who took my offense, "this one thing I do, forgetting those things which are behind, and reaching forth unto those things which are before" (Philippians 3:13).

You are my Jehovah Nissi (the lord My Banner), victor, and savior who has cleared the path for me. Proverbs 3:6 tells me that if in all my ways I acknowledge You, You will direct my paths. I therefore acknowledge You as Jehovah Sabaoth (the lord of Hosts), Lord Almighty, King of Glory, El Shaddai (God Almighty) the All-sufficient One, and El Olam (Everlasting God).

You are God over eternal things and Lord over my life. Amen.